DinoZone
TYRANNOSAURUS REX

KATIE WOOLLEY

WINDMILL
BOOKS

Published in 2017 by **Windmill Books**, an Imprint of Rosen Publishing
29 East 21st Street, New York, NY 10010

Author: Katie Woolley
Designers: Neal Cobourne and Emma Randall
Editors: Joe Harris and Anna Brett

Picture credits: Cover illustration: Rudolf Farkas. Interior illustrations: Arcturus Image Library
(Stefano Azzalin: 4t, 13, 15b, 17; Martin Bustamante: 5, 6, 14, 16, 18, 23, 29; Juan Calle: 8, 11, 20,
24; Mat Edwards: 28; Rudolf Farkas: 19, 25; Colin Howard: 15t, 22) and Shutterstock: 4l, 4c, 4r,
26-27 (Key: b-bottom, t-top, c-center, l-left, r-right).

Cataloging-in-Publication Data
Names: Woolley, Katie.
Title: Tyrannosaurus rex / Katie Woolley.
Description: New York : Windmill Books, 2017. | Series: Dinozone | Includes index.
Identifiers: ISBN 9781499481761 (pbk.) | ISBN 9781499481778 (library bound) |
  ISBN 9781508192886 (6 pack)
Subjects: LCSH: Tyrannosaurus rex--Juvenile literature.
Classification: LCC QE862.S3 W66 2017 | DDC 567.912'9--dc23

Manufactured in the United States of America
CPSIA Compliance Information: Batch #BW17PK: For Further Information contact Rosen Publishing, New York, New York at 1-800-237-9932

CONTENTS

What are dinosaurs? 4

T. rex: The most famous dinosaur of all 6

The world of *T. rex*...........................8

What did *T. rex* look like? 10

Tremendous teeth............................ 12

Hunter or scavenger? 14

A fierce fighter.............................. 16

Super senses................................ 18

Young *T. rex* 20

How do we know about
Tyrannosaurus rex? 22

Famous fossils 24

T. rex's world............................... 26

Myths About *T. rex* 28

Glossary 30

Further information 31

Index....................................... 32

What are dinosaurs?

Dinosaurs were reptiles that walked the Earth for 165 million years, long before there were any humans. We know of about 700 types of dinosaurs. But scientists think there were at least 1,500.

Tyrannosaurus rex

Triceratops

Prehistoric plant

Dinosaurs such as *Triceratops* (try-SEH-rah-tops) ate plants. The plant eaters were hunted and eaten by meat eaters such as *Tyrannosaurus rex* (ty-RAH-noh-sore-us REX).

Huayangosaurus
(hoy-YAN-goh-SORE-us)

Fast Facts

The scientist Richard Owen first used the word "dinosaur" in 1842. This was over 170 years ago!

Huayangosaurus' plates protected it from meat eaters.

Dinosaur means "terrible lizard."

5

T. rex: The most famous dinosaur of all

Tyrannosaurus rex was a truly fearsome dinosaur. It had long, razor-sharp teeth and a powerful bite. Measuring 39 feet (12 m) from tip to tail, it was as long as a bus!

T. rex could be up to 20 feet (6 m) tall. That's more than three times as tall as an adult human.

Compared to its huge body, *T. rex's* arms were tiny! They were only about 3 feet (1 m) long.

About 30 *Tyrannosaurus rex* fossils have been found, but none are complete. Scientists think this prehistoric monster had about 200 bones. However, nobody knows exactly how many.

Fast Facts

When: Late Cretaceous period

Food: Other dinosaurs

Size: 39 feet (12 m) long

←You!

Weight: 7.7 tons (7,000 kg)

How it moved: On two legs

Found in: Canada and United States

"T. rex" is short for *Tyrannosaurus rex*. It means **"tyrant lizard king."**

The world of *T. rex*

Tyrannosaurus rex roamed the Earth during the Cretaceous period, about 65 million years ago. It lived in a part of the world that is now North America.

At that time, North America was warm and humid. *T. rex* lived in forests near big rivers. It spent much of its time hunting among the trees.

Fast Facts
The Cretaceous period lasted about 79 million years. It was longer than the Triassic and Jurassic periods.

Many other dinosaurs lived alongside *T. rex*. It shared its world with other well-known dinosaurs such as *Iguanodon*, *Ankylosaurus*, *Triceratops*, and *Maiasaura*.

Iguanodon

Ankylosaurus

What did T. rex look like?

T. rex had a huge, heavy head, balanced by a long, stiff tail. Its skull alone was over 5 feet (1.5 m) long. Its tail made up about half the length of its body.

T. rex was built for running quickly after its prey. Its powerful legs ended with claws that could hold down prey. Its sharp teeth were the perfect weapons to tear into flesh!

Heavy tail

Big, sharp teeth

Short arms

Strong back legs

T. rex had three toes, but only two fingers.

Claws

10

Fast Facts

The eyeball of a *T. rex* was the size of a human adult's fist!

Was this mighty meat eater brown, green, or red? Was it striped or spotted? Unless a fossil of *T. rex's* skin is found, we will never know for sure. Some scientists even think that *T. rex* had feathers!

A *T. rex* with feathers might have looked like this.

Tremendous teeth

Tyrannosaurus rex's jaws contained 60 sharp teeth. Each tooth was as long as a human hand! Its bite was three times more powerful than a lion's. No other land animal has ever bitten that hard.

T. rex's jaws were 4 feet (1.2 m) long! That's the size of a 7-year-old child.

T. rex could hack away huge chunks of meat and crush bones as it ate. It could easily tear off 500 pounds (230 kg) of flesh in a single bite. That's the weight of a large pig.

With its long skull and wide jaws, *T. rex* may even have swallowed small dinosaurs whole!

Fast Facts

When one of *T. rex's* teeth broke, a new one simply grew in its place.

Hunter or scavenger?

Some scientists think that *Tyrannosaurus rex* hunted and killed most of the meat that it ate, like a lion. Others think that it mostly scavenged dead or dying dinosaurs, like a hyena.

T. rex used its good sense of smell to find food. It may have driven other predators away from their meals. They would have been scared away by the size of this mighty dinosaur.

From fossil finds, we know that *T. rex* ate horned dinosaurs, such as *Triceratops*, and duck-billed dinosaurs, such as *Maiasaura*.

Triceratops

Maiasaura lived in large herds. *T. rex* probably picked off old or sick animals.

Maiasaura

Fast Facts

When food was scarce, *T. rex* would turn on each other! *T. rex* bones have been found in the stomachs of other *T. rex*.

A fierce fighter

T. rex probably hunted alone. Its size meant that *T. rex* was big enough to take on large dinosaurs. It may have even attacked huge sauropods, such as *Alamosaurus* (AH-lah-moh-SORE-us)!

Alamosaurus

Fast Facts

T. rex was one of the dinosaurs that inspired the movie character, Godzilla!

We know from fossils that *Tyrannosaurus rex* sometimes lived together. However, we also know that these enormous reptiles often fought each other.

Many *Tyrannosaurus rex* skeletons have bite marks from the teeth of other *T. rex*. They probably fought over food, territory, or mates.

The most famous *T. rex* fossil, "Sue," has bite marks on her face from another *T. rex*.

Super senses

All dinosaurs relied on their senses to help them find food and avoid predators. *T. rex* was one of the best predators due to three of its five senses being very well developed.

T. rex often hunted at night when it was hidden from its prey by the dark. It used its super sense of smell to locate prey before attacking. We know its smell was good because fossils show the area around the part of the brain responsible for smell was large.

T. rex's brain was larger than the brains of other dinosaurs that had a similar body size.

Fast Facts

We don't know about *T. rex's* sense of taste or touch as its tongue and skin haven't survived in fossil form like its bones have.

Scientists know about *T. rex's* smell, sight and hearing by studying fossils.

T. rex's eyeballs were huge and it is believed that they grew bigger with age. Forward-facing eyes worked together to see images and gave *T. rex* a good range of vision, unlike plant-eating dinosaurs whose eyes were on the sides of their heads and worked separately.

By studying the ear bones of a *T. rex*, scientists know that it could hear a range of sounds. It was good at hearing low rumbles which helped it track the movement of prey in the distance.

Young T. rex

T. rex started out as an egg, which hatched into a baby dinosaur. No fossils of *T. rex* eggs have ever been found, so we don't know what exact size or shape they would have been.

Young *T. rex* grew quickly. By the age of 14 it weighed as much as a baby elephant.

2 years old　　　　**14 years old**　　　　**25 years old**

It's possible a mother *T. rex* stayed with its young when they were small and vulnerable to attack. *T. rex* mothers probably taught their young how to hunt. As they grew up, they would start hunting on their own.

Fast Facts

Some scientists think that young *T. rex* had feathers, which disappeared as it grew up.

Young T. rex

Young T. rex

Mother T. rex

How do we know about *Tyrannosaurus rex*?

By looking at fossils, scientists can learn about *T. rex's* body, the way it lived, and the world around it.

The first *T. rex* fossil was discovered in 1902 by a famous fossil hunter called Barnum Brown. He dug it up in Montana. Since then, *T. rex* fossils have been found in Canada, the United States, and Mongolia.

Canada

USA

Mongolia

You can see *T. rex* skeletons at many natural history museums.

For a long time, people thought that *T. rex* was the biggest meat-eating dinosaur. Now, we have found fossils from some other predators, such as *Spinosaurus*, that were even bigger.

Skull

Neck

Spine

Hips

Tail

Teeth

Jaw

Arm

Ribs

Leg

Fast Facts
T. rex was named in 1905 by Henry Fairfield Osborn.

By looking at *T. rex's* skull, scientists can find out about its brain. They say that *T. rex* was fairly smart for a dinosaur.

Famous fossils

Many *T. rex* fossils have been given nicknames. The largest fossil is called "Sue." She is 39 feet (12 m) long and 12 feet (3.6 m) high.

In 2001, the most complete *T. rex* fossil was found. The bones belonged to a juvenile *T. rex*, nicknamed "Jane." At 20 feet (6 m), she is just half the length of Sue.

"Sue"

"Jane"

Fast Facts

Sue is named after Sue Hendrickson, the paleontologist who discovered her in 1990.

Sue would have been really fearsome, even for a *T. rex*! From looking at her fossil, scientists can tell that she had been in a lot of fights. Sue was about 28 years old when she died. She is the oldest *Tyrannosaurus rex* that we know about.

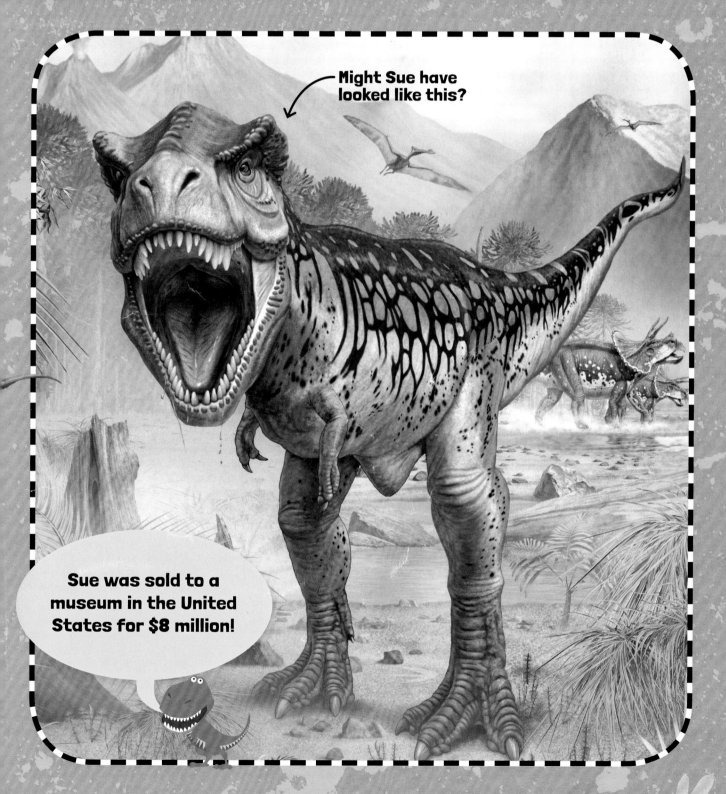

Might Sue have looked like this?

Sue was sold to a museum in the United States for $8 million!

T. rex's world

Parasaurolophus

Centrosaurus

Maiasaura

Triceratops

NORTH
AMERICA

Carcharondontosaurus

Ankylosaurus

SOUTH
AMERICA

Saltasaurus

Tyrannosaurus rex

Giganotosaurus

Tyrannosaurs rex lived during the late Cretaceous period. Here are some dinosaurs that existed at the same time.

Iguanodon

Tarbosaurus

Spinosaurus

EUROPE

ASIA

Velociraptor

AFRICA

Oviraptor

AUSTRALIA

Dinosaurs have been found on every continent.

ANTARCTICA

Myths About *T. rex*

There are a lot of tall tales about *T. rex*! The truth might surprise you.

T. rex lived during the Jurassic period.

False! In fact, it lived millions of years later, during the late Cretaceous period.

T. rex was the biggest meat-eating dinosaur.

False! *T. rex* was a top predator, but it wasn't the biggest meat-eating dinosaur that ever lived.

T. rex could run as fast as a car!

False! It's unlikely that *T. rex* could run at 30 miles (48 km) per hour. It was more like 12–18 miles (19–29 km) per hour.

T. rex was green.

Maybe! We don't know what its skin looked like.

T. rex was smart!

False! It was smarter than its prey ... but most dinosaurs were not very intelligent.

T. rex could only see you if you moved.

False! *T. rex* had great eyesight. It would have spotted you, even standing still!

Glossary

attack To act aggressively.

Cretaceous period A period in Earth's history, between 144 and 65 million years ago.

fierce Violent, aggressive, or ferocious.

fossil The remains or imprint of an animal or plant, preserved for millions of years, now turned to stone.

hatch To emerge from an egg.

herd A group of animals living together.

humid Having a lot of moisture in the air.

hunter An animal that searches and kills its prey.

Jurassic period A time in Earth's history, between 206 and 144 million years ago.

juvenile A young animal, older than a baby.

mate The partner of an animal.

paleontologist A person who studies fossils.

predator An animal that eats other animals.

prey An animal that is eaten by other animals.

reptile An animal that has cold blood, lays eggs and has skin covered with scales or hard parts.

roam To move around a large area of land.

sauropods Large, plant-eating dinosaurs with long necks and tails.

scavenger An animal that searches for and collects food.

scientist A person who studies the way that the world works.

skeleton A frame made up of all the bones in an animal's body.

territory An area of land that an animal lives within and defends.

Triassic period A period in Earth's history, between 248 and 206 million years ago.

vulnerable Open to attack, easily hurt.

weapon A tool that is used to attack.

Further information

Further reading

Dinosaurs: A Spotter's Guide by editors of Weldon Owen (Weldon Owen, 2016)

First Encyclopedia of Dinosaurs and Prehistoric Life by Sam Taplin (Usborne, 2011)

iDinosaur by Darren Naish (Carlton Kids, 2014)

The T. Rex Handbook by Julius T. Csotonyi (Applesauce Press, an imprint of Sterling Publishing, 2016)

What's So Special about T. rex? by Nicky Dee (Dragonfly Group Ltd, 2016)

Why Did T. Rex Have Short Arms? And Other Questions About Dinosaurs by Melissa Stewart (Sterling, 2014)

Websites

For web resources related to the subject of this book, go to: **www.windmillbooks.com/weblinks** and select this book's title.

Index

A
Alamosaurus 16
Ankylosaurus 9, 26
arms 6, 10

B
bite 6, 12, 17
bones 7, 12, 15, 18, 19
brain 18, 23
Brown, Barnum 22

C
Carcharondontosaurus 26
Centrosuarus 26
claws 10
continent 27
Cretaceous period 7, 8, 28

E
egg 20
elephant 20
eye 19
  eyeball 11, 19
  eyesight 29

F
feathers 11, 21
fossils 7, 11, 17, 18, 20, 22, 23, 24, 25
  Jane 24
  Sue 17, 24, 25

G
Giganotosaurus 26
Godzilla 16

H
hearing 18, 19
herds 15
Huayangosaurus 5
hyena 14

I
Iguanodon 9, 27

J
jaws 12, 13
Jurassic period 8, 28

L
lion 14

M
Maiasaura 9, 15, 26
meat eaters 4, 5, 23, 28
museum 22, 25

O
Osborn, Henry Fairfield 23
Oviraptor 27

P
paleontologist 24
Parasaurolophus 26
plant eaters 4, 19
plates 5

S
Saltasaurus 26
sauropods 16
scientists 4, 5, 7, 11, 18, 21
sight 18
skin 11, 18, 29
skull 10, 13, 18, 23
smell 14, 18
Spinosaurus 23, 27

T
tail 10
Tarbosaurus 27
teeth 6, 10, 12, 13, 17
Triassic period 8
Triceratops 4, 9, 15, 26

V
Velociraptor 27